# Rowing with Wings

Books by James Harms

*Comet Scar*
*What to Borrow, What to Steal*
*After West*
*Freeways and Aqueducts*
*Quarters*
*The Joy Addict*
*Modern Ocean*

Limited editions and chapbooks

*Racheland*
*Animals in Distress & Pluto (stories)*
*Double Nickels on the Dime*
*East of Avalon*
*L.A. Afterglow*

# Rowing with Wings

poems by
James Harms

Carnegie Mellon University Press
Pittsburgh 2017

# Acknowledgments

My thanks to the editors of the following journals, magazines, anthologies, etc., where the poems in this book first appeared, often in earlier versions and occasionally with different titles:

*Aethlon* ("Koufax/Clemente"), *Barrow Street* ("Umbrella"), *Cave Wall* ("Phoebe at 8"), *Connotation Press* ("The Werewolves of Our Youth"), *The Cortland Review* ("The Gods"), *Diode* ("Auden in Winter," "Like Light"), *The Eberly College Magazine* ("Kennedy Wins West Virginia!"), *Ecotone* ("Where Is My Tree House?"), *The Gettysburg Review* ("When I First Met Your Mother"), *The Hampden-Sydney Poetry Review* ("A Good Day," "We Fell into the Sky"), *Hayden's Ferry Review* ("Ever Always"), *The Idaho Review* ("Apology Accepted," "The Goodbye Train," "Racheland"), *The Missouri Review* ("Aubade (Lisa Lisa Lisa)"), *A Narrow Fellow* ("Divorce Dream"), *The Northern Virginia Review* ("Auden in Winter (by Avedon)"), *Ping-Pong* ("Daedalus Beach"), *Shenandoah* ("New Moon Economy"), *Southern Humanities Review* ("The Only Lie Worth Telling"), *The 2River View* ("Accidental Bohemian," "From My Lips"), *Quarterly West* ("After Surrender," "Other Summers"), *Valparaiso Poetry Review* ("Accidental Happiness"), *West Branch* ("Is He Our Half-Brother, Phoebe Asked, to Which Walt Raised His Right Hand and Said, He's Too Whole to Be Half of Anything").

"Phoebe at 8" was reprinted in the *Alhambra Poetry Calendar 2010*. "New Moon Economy" was reprinted on *Poetry Daily*. "Kennedy Wins West Virginia!" was reprinted in *Eyes Burning at the Edge of the Woods: Fiction and Poetry from West Virginia*.

My endless thanks to Caroline Mulry, Laura Kasischke, and Jeff Carpenter, without whom it's difficult to imagine things being as good as they are . . . and to Lisa Di Bartolomeo for helping me start over. Also, my deepest gratitude to John Hoppenthaler, David Wojahn, Paige Muendel, and Paula McLain for their many years of support and friendship, and to Paula again for reading the manuscript of this book so well and helping me revise it; and to Gerald Costanzo,

Cynthia Lamb, and Linda Warren for their sustaining belief in my
work. Thank you to my students and colleagues at West Virginia
University.

To my mother, in memory, thank you, thank you, thank you. Thanks
also to my father, Richard, and my stepfather, Gene; my brother,
Tom; and my sister, Marianne, also in memory. I've already thanked
my sister Carrie but I'll do it again since there could never be enough
thanks for her.

The "Auden in Winter" poems were inspired by the 1960 bromide
print of Auden by Richard Avedon, National Portrait Gallery,
London.

The following songs and songwriters inspired the poems that borrow
their titles: "When I First Met Your Ma" by Paul Kelly; "Apology
Accepted" by The Go-Betweens; "Racheland" by The Jazz Butcher;
"The Goodbye Train" by The Apartments (Peter Milton Walsh);
"Only Lie Worth Telling" by Paul Westerberg; "Good Day" by Paul
Westerberg; "Maria's Little Elbows" by Sparklehorse; "From My Lips"
by Grant McLennan.

ABOUT THE BOOK

The text of Rowing with Wings is set in Hightower (1994), and
Gotham (2000), both designed by Tobias Frere-Jones. This book was
designed by Linda Warren at Studio Deluxe, Culver City, California.
It was printed and bound by Jeff Carpenter of Westcott Press,
Altadena, California.

Library of Congress Control Number 2017937496
ISBN 978-0-88748-626-5
Copyright ©2017 by James Harms
All rights reserved
Printed and bound in the United States of America

10 9 8 7 6 5 4 3 2 1

# Contents

FOR WALT, PHOEBE AND DASH:
POETRY BEGINS WITH THE THREE OF YOU

*And now they pause on that hill where Dedalus,*
*At the end of his flight, first fluttered to earth:*
*He had risked himself to the sky, away and afloat*
*To the north, through the cold air, unprecedented,*
*Rowing with wings—which he then dedicated*
*To you, Phoebus Apollo, there on the spot*
*Where he landed, and built in your honour*
*A mighty temple, the doors of it decorated*
*With scenes in relief. . . .*
*You too would figure significantly,*
*Icarus, had sorrow allowed it. Twice*
*Dedalus tried to model your fall in gold, twice*
*His hands, the hands of a father, failed him.*

—VIRGIL, *AENEID BOOK VI*
TR. SEAMUS HEANEY

**ONE**
AFTER SURRENDER

## Phoebe at 8

You fell asleep by the river. I walked back
carrying you, your sandals hooked in my fingers.
The glow of stardust on leaves lingered
in-between the black of sky and the black

of earth. I drove while you slept, wondering
if with you I'd ever run out of chances.
At the corner Texaco near home you danced
around the car washing windows to the wandering

bass line of "I Thank You." I filled the tank
and tried to remember the words, the song
nailed in place to 1968, the wrong
year as it turned out to think about thanks.

You were unimagined, unknowable then.
I was exactly your age, as free as I've ever been.

# After Surrender

*to Paige on her 35th birthday*

What I remember most about Bob Marley
    is from a poem by William Matthews,
how his widow carried his hair home in a box
    on her lap, the plane bucking in the warm
Caribbean updrafts. In a dream
    he walks up to my car stuck in traffic and says,
*Just follow me through the meadows,*
    though the meadows are wrecked with tires
and broken furniture, the ready refuse of empires.
    And now I'm wondering if it isn't Dean's dream
since I know he's a had a few about Marley,
    and where, really, does my life end
and another's begin? at the edge of dreams?
    I was on a bus in Austria just leaving
Salzburg when I heard Marley had died.
    I didn't know his music well, had never heard
"Exodus" or "Pimper's Paradise," just Clapton
    and Johnny Nash, their capable covers.
So it's not as though I loved him yet,
    but still: the air seemed to thicken in my throat
as I tried to catch my breath. Now what?
    It's your birthday. You're a year younger
than Marley was when he died, and you've moved
    on from us, if *on* is a place two blocks away.
I know we can't, but let's share a bottle of wine,
    watch the news, see if snow will close
the schools tomorrow. You met Bill Matthews once—
    just a year or two into our marriage,
and you've heard me talk about my dreams
    of Marley, how Bill still seems to speak
from another room, a broken phrase or two,
    that "poetry teaches us a certain ordinary bravery,"

though Marley's was a little more than that.
    But now I'm sure it was my dream, my memory,
my fear. You remember my fear.
    After surrender is the negotiation of borders,
the division of spoils, the new road
    suddenly within the other's territory.
From where I sit, two blocks and several
    years away, I can see your country,
especially when you sleep. And *your* dreams:
    smoke rising from a battlefield, smoke
hanging in the air between us.

## Where Is My Tree House?

After all those years collecting lumber, I wake
and find it gone, the view from my bedroom
so woeful and unobstructed, no cabin floating
in the limbs, no cottage in the morning air.
How I loved it. I remember struggling
the old sofa up the trunk and squeezing it
through the door. My parents didn't care,
never noticed the cable snaking from their
window or saw the blue glow of the ten-inch
I bought on time from El Gordo on the corner,
who threw in a dime bag for free. O, the narrow
chimney made of bricks borrowed from the Fenley's
crumbling wall, the wax paper windowpanes.
I'd suspect Derek, but Derek's in jail.
If Jay weren't dead, he'd have done it for sure.
I tried not to steal any nails or joists; I used
one hammer I found in the hedge, and a saw
I returned each day to my uncle's tool chest.
I *did* lift and change the phrase in line four above
("a dwelling in the evening air"), but he's
dead too. It took twelve years to build
and my children planned to live there one day.
I would say I'm sorry to them but lately
they snarl and spit when I enter the room.
I named a comet one night while sitting
on its roof counting stars. 8,124 before
I gave up. The comet left a scar right here.
If you want to know its name, give it back.

# Other Summers

When my son couldn't sleep after hours
of throwing up, his belly as tight

as a full sail, he lay on me through the night
so we made a cross with our bodies
or an X: "It doesn't hurt so much

this way," he said. And when I woke every hour
or two I'd see his eyes open to moonlight,

the curtains drawn, sash raised to early summer
in West Virginia, where sounds of digging fill in
every silence. We listened together in our separate

thoughts, his of breakfast, when he might at last
eat again ("Cheerios and an egg, please"),

mine of other summers, the distant sizzle
of waves lathering wet sand, hours diving
for abalone and lobster, the gravity

of sunlight pulling me to the surface; I heard
I'm sure the bubbles of my own emerging breath,

the whistle I learned to issue as I ascended.
The Pacific delivered its slow insinuations
until I realized they were his thoughts

not mine, the frying egg sizzling, a dream
inside of Walt, a dream sighing from his body.

His eyes were closed, stomach calm at last,
all that peace in a tangle of sheets, so much peace
in what we don't know yet, haven't learned,

can't quite figure out, the peace of toys
and tended baths, the peace of living

instead of remembering. To Walt,
the distant digging was a cricket's chirp, a lullaby.
He couldn't hear the picks, couldn't see

the coal, black as water at the bottom
of the sea, couldn't feel the gravity of other summers.

But at forty-four, at last,
I hushed the west inside me, listened instead
to Walt's dreams. And I slept.

# Ever Always

Was I ever a child?
I played (I'm sure
of it) with Philip
and Lee in the center
of the schoolyard.

I loved
the leather balls
and the box
of jacks and
I hugged Philip
too hard.

I tried to let
her see me,
Louise, but she
dropped her glasses
and stepped on them
and ground the lenses
with her heel
as if to say
I will never see you.
(Her name was not
Louise but I
can't say her name.)

And I was never a child
but why must we
why have we
stopped playing?

How far away it is,
the center of
always, the schoolyard.

Where
is Philip? Where
is Lee?

# When I First Met Your Mother

*to Phoebe*

Maybe it's hard for you
to imagine I ever loved her,
that one day I watched
from across Third Avenue
as she rolled her apron and tucked it
in her coat pocket, looked up
and down the block for me
then lit a cigarette and let
her head drift up and away
as if hearing Marvin Gaye –
she always lost a little
gravity listening to "I Want You."
I finished my beer without
calling out, just watched her
wait for me from across the street,
her shift over at last
and the hours already
beginning to narrow.
But that was later, years after
I walked into a room
in Armstrong Hall,
settled my papers
on the desk and looked up:
there was *Before Your Mother*
and *Everything After*;
the everything started then.
When I first met your mother,
she wore a man's silk shirt
over a camisole, and the sort of
flowing pants that seem made

of air or smoke, though they were
the yellow of old linen,
of a white sheet spread
in a field of mustard,
a picnic where I first
loved your mother.
But that, too, was later,
though I remember her face
above me, how it seemed
held like a chip of sea glass
to the sun, the sky beyond
so empty of anything
it seemed filled to spilling over
with blue, a color like the hum
you once whispered to your dolls,
your plush bears and ponies,
the sound of your singing
softening the end of love.

## Auden in Winter (by Avedon)

On St. Mark's Place, Auden
has stepped from his apartment
into the falling snow
wearing a topcoat and shabby
shoes, though he's forgotten
to put on his socks or has decided
not to, the portrait by Avedon
less a sitting than a snapshot
of time. By 1960,
Auden has suffered more from love
than war, lived in books
instead of life, or so sayeth
his many critics who wonder
"what's become of Wystan?"
His poems now talk when they
need to sing, which is to say
they seem sure of themselves,
happy to hum between avowals,
though most of this comes from
those too envious to trust.
What if the poems simply
understand something (always
a danger), perhaps
what to do with suffering
or how to suffer less?
They remind me a bit
of Bill Murray: a little rueful,
not so much sure of anything
as resigned to *something*:
resignation in the midst
of wonder. It occurs to me
that Bill Murray is beginning

to look like Auden,
and that suffering itself
is a sort of knowing. Or perhaps
it's learning not knowing,
a slow erosion instead of
a solid cliff face, a slow erosion
of wonder. Or is that true
only for those who step onto
a sidewalk covered in snow
as if into a field stretching
all the way to nothing—
a nothing that is or was or might
someday be. But that's
the business of faith not poetry,
and Auden is clear on that
in a way that Stevens will never
own: it's people, not nothing,
who pass on their suffering.
And so we leave it all behind
or learn to live with the loss, with
what can't be forgotten, however
beneficent the forgiveness.
The ever-growing past:
a far horizon slowly blurring
to white, to erasure and silence.
Still, it's the learning-to-live-with
that is so difficult. But that's me
talking, not Auden.

## Maria's Little Elbows

She sleeps sideways
when she sleeps, which isn't often.
On Sunday mornings
she likes the bells and scuffle
of hard soles along the sidewalk
below my bedroom window,
and on Wednesdays
the wheeze of the double doors
of my little boy's school bus
arriving at the corner—
she likes to listen
in her sleep, when she sleeps,
sleeping sideways.
And so
I sleep sideways, too,
when Maria comes to visit.
I remember my little boy
singing along
when she sang her one song,
*loneliness* its one word every other
measure like a hesitant mantra
stuttering its way to peace,
her little pill-derived piece of peace.
My Maria and her small
sweet kisses, like the surprises
I hide for my little boy
in his lunch box:
a caramel wrapped
in a paper napkin;
the quarter in a plastic bag
so he can buy a carton of punch
from the lunch lady
in a hairnet.
My little boy loves
Maria and helps me sweeten
her coffee with milk we stir

full of brown sugar and
cinnamon; we whisper
in the kitchen as we heat
and swirl a whirlpool
of brown and white, until
it slowly softens to beige, to
*palomino* says my little boy
for his favorite horse.
And we take it to Maria
sleeping sideways in my bed
on Sunday morning.
My little boy watches
while she dreams;
he whispers, *She is worth
hundreds of sparrows.*
And on Thursdays when
he is with his mother
I wake sideways next to Maria
and wish
well never mind:
my Maria, my little boy,
my perfectly delimited life.

**TWO**

THE GOODBYE TRAIN

## We Fell into the Sky

And when I returned
you stayed deep
in the blue as if
folded with flour
in a deep, blue bowl,
as if blended with
light and clouds.
And because, as always,
I neglected to look behind,
knowing I was loved,
I never noticed
you hadn't followed.
How is it Orpheus
was punished for his doubt,
I for my certainty?

## Apology Accepted

And there it was:
*I'm sorry* scrawled in lipstick
on my bathroom mirror, and again:
sketched in nail polish on the face
of my watch. What did she
do? I asked the air surrounding
a biscuit tin (within which
was a possible breakfast
if she'd left me anything).
*Exactly*, said the little voice
I carry near my heart—I hear it
breathe when it has no opinions,
little bellows of used air there
in my breast pocket, polishing
my Parker pen like an
exhalation on the glass
of a cell phone. *You don't know*,
it said. *But everyone else does.* Oh
well, I thought. The end
is nearly always punctuated
by shame disguised as apology,
as if I'm *sorry* is an antidote
for the quiet surrounding a lie.
But I woke this morning
confused by beauty, some bird
singing on the windowsill.
O, nightingale or whatever
you are, let me empty my stale
regrets into the four notes
you vary and repeat, let me . . .
oops. I see now: one leg is missing,
caught in the window or swatted

off by Miss Kitty. But sing on,
sweet thing, sing your sorrow
or you're sorry. *But why should
it be sorry*, my little voice asks, *and
why are YOU sorry?* Shut up!
I say. Suffering is a sacred thing
Or is that forgiveness, yes,
Forgiveness is a sacred thing!
I stuff a handkerchief in my pocket.
And you are due, my sweet sweet
bird, my one-legged
are you a finch? due a break,
clear skies, a little blue in the maw
of a cat-shaped cloud.
A little blue. Me, too. Me, too.

## Umbrella

I woke one morning
and she wasn't there
which wasn't new: she
needed those nights with
her friends, her time to
feel herself as herself, not
someone married to
an umbrella in a life of
sunny days, Mr. Shadow-
maker, Mr. Good Guy.
Our son was awake early
as usual, and I'd just
set him up with a glass
of juice and Sponge
Bob when I heard her
trip on the landing.
I looked up and saw her
face rising with each stair,
the smeared mascara,
the sliding smile. She
said, I'll take care of him,
go back to bed, and she
put her phone on the
nightstand and stumbled
over a stack of folded
laundry as she lurched
back to our boy watching
TV in the next room.
"Just fucked," we used
to call it, that look at
the end of a long night

of long beers and
longer bourbons, the long
want of self-pity disguised
as love. Sweet Narcissus,
here's your face in a
puddle of moonlight,
the poem rising like bile
in the back of my throat,
the new aubade in a time
of plenty. I dropped back
into bed. As if to sleep
again in the breath of first
light might dissolve a simple
look, *her* look at the top
of the stairs. So I took her
phone in hand and thought
No, it isn't right, but then
it was. And I read the record
of a long night, her texts and his
from evening into early morning,
mostly sexts, dull or dumb or
simply drunk, and then
a lie to me followed by one
to her best friend, until
it ended at his apartment:
"Open your door," she typed
in the last text, 4:05 a.m.
And the silence between
that moment and when
I sat there shaking, her phone
in my hand, my wife still drunk
and just fucked in the next
room holding my young son
as she fell into sleep, Sponge
Bob complaining to Patrick
about crabby patties and jelly

fish, the weight of water
in a world without air . . . I sat
in that silence, that space,
and struggled for breath
and wondered what next:
how to breathe again
at the bottom of this new sea.

# The Goodbye Train

No one would ever call you
a *melancholy Jane*. Or even June.

Your smile is a butterfly
stunned to stone in the ruins.

You always seem to be saying
hello. And so hello is a train

disappearing in its own steam.
Goodbye, Hello. *Again,*

*please*, you tell your little girl,
who wants to stop drawing flowers.

You catch her staring out
the window. For an hour

she's been staring out the window.
Your smile is a seam slowly

splitting on your face. *What's there?*
you ask your little girl, who knows

enough to shake her head, to shrug
hard against the air pressing down

on her shoulders. You make a wish,
then kiss her flinch into a frown.

Outside the deer nibble your nasturtium,
not knowing the taste will hurt them.

## Racheland

No stories, said the wren
hiding in my wings, I'm sick
of stories. So I kissed her.
And the touch of
lips on bone was like
the fragrance of perfume
in a phone booth: Finally
the sweetness, however
used, someone's secondhand
smell like a gently rotting
pear at the bottom of
the bowl, disassembling like
her last face falling apart
in her hands as she knelt
at the curb and touched
her tongue to feel
the prayer.
She fell apart for me. She
held a part of me to feel
it stiffen like a story, a lie
that hardens into paper.
She wrote her name
on the inside of her wrist
(she told me this), as if
*Rachel* could button up
the vein. Her name
wasn't *Rachel* but I can't
say her name. And I've
never been an eagle
but I dropped
the wren into a cloud.
I kissed the space beneath

my wing and spoke
her name into that darkness
and felt the feathers
fill my throat in the thin air
so near heaven or whatever
she called it, perhaps
Racheland. Oh, Rachel.

## Koufax/Clemente

I.

In San Juan, in '65, every other person
wore a Pirates cap in honor of Clemente,
and my father was father to a flock
of lapsed Catholics and expatriate
Episcopalians, who took Communion
in Spanish, the sermon in English,
then gathered in the cathedral courtyard
for punch and rum-flavored flan.

*

My sisters and I ate our afternoon
snack in the kitchen and argued in two
languages. When it comes to *perfect*
there is little difference between English
and Spanish, just an "o" at the end like a small,
stunned exhalation, which is what my father
murmured one afternoon as he walked up
behind me and saw the headline over
my shoulder: "Oh."

My sister snatched the paper
from my hands and sang out the word
*Perfecto!* r's rolling like the trill of a warbler,
then *Koufax*, the name in the caption.
Dad shook his head, walked with a cup
of coffee toward his study door, and I
began to cry, as if a word said aloud
is a spoiled secret.

But in truth I couldn't read yet in Spanish
*or* English, had no idea what had happened
or what it meant, *perfecto*, or why the crowd
of players in the picture was lifting the man

to its shoulders. I just watched my father's
study door close behind him, the secret
swallowed back into silence.

*

When finally we went home to L.A.
in that glum summer of '68, my father
took my brother and me to Dodger games
every year or two until he moved away
to San Diego, "as far away as Venus,"
my little brother told our mom.
"Yes," she said. "Just about."

2.
On certain summer days my daughter sprints
across Clemente Bridge to pose beneath
the statue of that great man. She smiles
for the picture we'll send her grandfather,
who remembers the year the plane went down.

*

It's still warm and sweaty near the end
of the season, though we're snug
in the shade beneath the upper deck.
My oldest son has nodded off, the bill
of his faded blue cap angled low.
His little brother eats peanuts and drops
shells to the concrete floor then stomps
on them. Only my daughter watches the game,
still wearing her souvenir batting helmet,
the black and gold shining in the shade.

There's an empty seat beside her, another
between her brothers; I bought the tickets
months ago, before I knew. A cheer

goes up as Sauerkraut Saul wins
the Pierogi race at the end of the 5th inning—
I watch my daughter turn to say something
to her stepsister, who isn't there. She looks
around, and then at me, says, "Sorry, you lose,"
and smiles because she isn't sorry:
it's my Dodgers who are going to lose,
and she's teasing me, two empty seats or not.
We touch cups: her Sprite, my Yuengling.

*

From anywhere in PNC Park you can see
boats on the Allegheny, the other bridges
beyond Clemente's: Rachel Carson,
Andy Warhol, the new heroes of Pittsburgh, PA.
I find myself watching the river, the traffic
downtown, the way the world keeps moving
even on game day.

I reach across the empty seat and knock
the plastic of my daughter's batting helmet.
She pretends to slap my hand away,
then holds it, laughs. "Oh, Dad," she says,
which I still am.

# Daedalus Beach

1.
A red flag has torn loose of the lifeguard tower and wrapped
his mother like a dress. Then again, all memory is pixilated,
just wind hiss and wave blur, sand pitting the lens until his
father gives up, walks south forever, drops the camera on the
beach. *Sleep*, whispers the sea. It always does. And he wishes
he were worn out, singed at the edges. When he awakens
he's the only one left in the world, immortal as the song in a
seashell. His song. But then the sudden face in the crook of his
arm. She sings. He sings. And then it starts all over again.

2.
He found his mother in his dream
waist-deep and walking toward
the waves, her clothes growing
heavy, her gray hair thin and flat
against her forehead, eyes and
mouth open to the sea. He called
to her from shore, he tried
to remove his wings, to swim
to her, the feathers dragging
behind him, waves pushing him
back, fighting what little flight
was possible. The wings
were useless. He called to her.
He shook himself. He tried
to wake up. He watched her
until she wasn't there, the empty
waves rolling forward, the sea
and its little kites of sunlight,
the sea all sadness and certainty.
He watched the sea now

that there was no one else
to watch. And he waited to
awaken. And he never did.

# Auden in Winter

In 1960, W. H. Auden was still
in love with Chester Kallman,
still living part-time in his mind
and the rest of the year
on St. Mark's Place with Chester,
who'd broken it off in 1941.
What I have learned from this
is how hard it is to love
from a beachhead dug in air.
What I have learned from this
is not to love or live with your betrayer.
Still, it seems reasonable to do
something with the betrayal.

In 1960, in Avedon's photograph,
the snow surrounded Auden
like pale apostrophes
or quote marks enclosing silence.
And silence isn't nothing
or nothingness, just as nobody believes
poetry makes nothing happen,
unless it's the nothing that is.
When I was betrayed
over and over—my wife with
her rolled up newspaper
teaching me to mind—
each lie was a sort of silence,
since the noise of words led
to static, a sound in my mind
of dust swirling and footsteps
over ground glass,
as if a veldt or salt flat
had unrolled within me
filling all my empty spaces
with nothing. In 1960,

on St. Mark's Place, Auden
stood ankle-deep in drifts
to let Avedon play with time.
Of course the stillness is a fiction,
however fixed in silver and silence:
In a few months, I will be born
at the other edge of the continent,
and in 13 years, Auden will die
in Vienna, with Chester in sight.
Clocks are like invaded countries—
they stop and then, in time,
start up again, new borders
like missing hours, enclosures
best left to the imagination.

In 1960, Auden was 53
and I was waiting to be born.
What was I waiting for in 1973?
The day he died was invisible
to time, or at least to
the instruments we use
to bottle seconds in amber
before storing them away.
I was 13 in '73, in love with
no one and nothing,
and, Oh, how I loved to hold
that nothing in my arms,
aware of Auden the way a boy
falls in love first with the look
of light creeping across
a classroom, and then with
the way the light haloes a face,
and then with a face
that time will wreck and ruin
though what that has to do
with love we're all waiting to learn.

**THREE**
GOOD DAY

# The Only Lie Worth Telling

*. . . is I'm in love with you.*

I like the way the ocean lies to the beach.
Or sunlight to a shadow.
The way the radio will lie
through rush hour traffic: *sweet lord, sweet thing,*
*sweet dreams are made of these.*

The lie wasn't the kiss, Judas said.
It was believing the money would make a difference.
And that it wouldn't.

I like the way the clouds lie
to the moon: *We'll clothe*
*your nakedness*, they say. Or how
they slide through winter trees as if
substantial enough to snag, how they
slip and whisper, *Please, hold me awhile.*

But it's a lie to be held
when you're turning into rain, a lie
to be held when thinking
of someone else.

The way the iceberg lies
to the ship, just a snow cone
floating abeam.

I love the way the mortician lies
to the corpse:
*You look beautiful lying there.*
He brushes her hair. A little
lipstick, the lightest rouge.

But *shh . . .* , he says. *Don't say a word,*
*you'll scare the children.  Better yet,*
*let me sew your lips shut.*

# The New Moon Economy

We've all been in towns
that wouldn't have us, whose woods
beyond the cemetery
hide houses made of leaves,
their windows lit low
by peat fires, the slow stink
of heat rising through trees
then sinking into grass, the mounds
that seem to shrug and settle.
And the exiles we are, in overcoats
and heavy shoes, we present
our sticky faces to the tellers
and soda jerks, the lovely girls
cracking gum at the luncheonettes,
and we're told to leave, simple
as that, told to walk our sorry selves
back to sea, back to sod, back
to wherever we come from which, funny
enough, is a place a lot like
this one, happy once and
lovely and now turned
like the moon to black.

## Divorce Dream

I found the lost grove
   I'd heard about
      in a vale beneath
a fallen cloud behind
   my grandfather's
      stables, and borrowed
his long-dead horse,
   a Palomino with
      a blaze of cream
between his eyes
   who wouldn't cross
      water, and rode
for hours down
   row after row
      of orange trees until
the cloud dissolved
   in tracts of houses.
      In one my children
quilted butterflies
   to extinction: the most
beautiful bedclothes.

# The Werewolves of Our Youth

Sinclair never wanted
to hurt anyone. He started out
the little brother to everyone's
best friend, which is
to say, a witness to beauty,
a beggar on the edge
of the in-crowd. And so
he took the moon seriously,
which is to say, personally,
awaking one winter night
in charge of his own
disappointment. What
started out a joyride
in his brother's graduation
present ended up
a robbery one town over,
the Dairy Mart in Fairmont;
he simply hit the small
Korean man four times
before reaching for
the cash register. And so
it began: transgression
the sweetest catalyst,
all the properties of moonlight
contained in a simple act—
which is to say,
he was changed, though
no one knew. Until
last Wednesday evening
when a woman's arm
was found two miles from
her armless body.
And Sinclair slept naked
in the culvert with the other

arm tucked beneath
his chin, partly gnawed on
and all pillow to
his happy dreams.
Unrecognizable in his armor
of fur, he loped off
at the sound of sirens.
No one saw him again.

# A Good Day

*doesn't have to be a Friday*
*doesn't need to be your birthday*
*is any day that you're alive*
                    –PAUL WESTERBERG

You meant to say
it was a good day,
the third one this week.
You'd slept well and long on the floor beside your bed, a boat
    of polished teak,
the sail from midnight
to daylight
a dream of blue distances
answering the bored benevolence
of prayer. A good day.
In fact, you intended to stay.
But evenings offend the lace of sunshine
still staining the highest pines.
The bridge glows orange in the bones of its ironwork.
You took it personally, the look
of light leaving through the western window,
the way even love can slow
to silence at dusk,
a good day gone to husks,
the air as gray and dry as chalk dust. You meant
to stay, to forget the spent
promises of fair weather and friendship.
Someone said they watched from across the bridge your lips
move as if in prayer. But you were reciting
your last text. And then you were typing
it into your phone, typing as you climbed over the railing:
    *Tell them I was tired.*
*Tell them all that I was tired.*

# Is He Our Half-Brother, Phoebe Asked, to Which Walt Raised His Right Hand and Said, He's Too Whole to Be Half of Anything

Dashiell tries so hard
to understand his mobile
& reach the plastic butterfly
& the red ladybug that
sings a little song when
its tail is tugged (do
ladybugs have tails?)
that most days he finds
the spot just beyond joy
& cries, so full of knowing
nothing he'll remember
that he has to let it go
& try again tomorrow.
The renewable world:
an answer to loss
that relies on losing.

## Kennedy Wins West Virginia!

He started out
a friend of Kennedy's,
though he started out
a Texan. Today
he swings
on the porch next
door and sings "Someone
to Watch Over Me"
as dusk thickens
in the street and
grays the day
down to shouts
and TV's mumbling
through open windows.
Twice he's talked
of Texas as all
horizon, the sort of
promise that slips
as evening wears away
the light, of coming here
to mountains so old
they ache and drift
beneath the weight
of sky, the way day
ends in hill shadow
and dust, smell of slag,
of water. He delivered
Hancock County
in a locked box, shook
JFK's hand, and
went home. But home
is an accident

of grace or birth,
is where you run out
of money or luck or find
yourself standing still
too long. LBJ sent him
back to West Virginia
and his wife Elaine
came with him; she liked
the virgin hemlocks,
the rhododendrons,
so they stayed.
He watches swallows
smoke from the glass
factory's cold chimney
and waits. Maybe home
is where purpose falls
in love with the light
settling in the trees
at dusk. LBJ called
once more to say
thanks, to say
Come on home. But Elaine
liked the chances
of her garden better here
than Texas, and there's
no horizon in these
mountains to remind him
of what's out of reach.
He likes to hear the roar
on Saturdays
from the stadium
across town, the crowd
noise bending in the silver
autumn air like
a train whistle entering
a tunnel. He likes

the way the river implies
an ending. So maybe
home is where we don't
mind ending, or don't
reach to flick on
the porch light
when evening falls
too early, the sun
surprised by the hills.
How easily
the hills surprise us.

## Accidental Bohemian

Slim boy on the sidewalk, you must be mine,
headphones locked to your ears as light leaves the earth
around you, day draining away like a voice calling you
in for dinner. You love the wind hiss at the edge of
song, the sweet leak of music that stains the air around
your body as your walk turns to dance on this quiet
street near home. I slow the car to keep pace, to stay
just behind and out of sight of you, to watch you sing
in a privacy so complete I'm called away, returned to
some central mind in the sky beyond your little brother's
small cloud (painted on blue paper and taped to the
refrigerator), where each of us is stilled in time and left
at the open door, beyond which are windows without
rooms, a place I'll always join you. Call it love.

# Auden in Winter

Auden in winter
under weather on St. Mark's Place, the sky collapsing
    around him.
Distance softens as it does in
early evening, snow brightening the coming
night like silver exposed to light. Auden visited

Isherwood in Brussels in 1938, and would
never have noticed then the end of landscape turning

white, Brueghel's Flanders disguised as Bethlehem.
In 1938 Flanders was a memory trying
not to recur,
trying not to make room in its crowded fields,
enough eternity for one century. But maybe not. In 1960
Richard Avedon counts seconds like snowflakes as the
    silver turns into Auden.

## Grownups Getting Drunk

Uncle Sal grills chicken while Mom and Dad
and Aunt Fiona sip heavy and slow on the side porch
and argue about the second yacht
on the left when you're sitting in the upstairs bar
at the Rusty Pelican in Newport Harbor: is it
David Crosby's or Mariah Carey's? And Sal
yells from his spot at the edge of the driveway
"Will you fucking get me a Tom Collins, Fiona!"
which has my cousin Ricky laughing like
a dumb genius reciting box scores to the deaf
kid pumping gas at the ARCO on Colorado Blvd.,
who's always there and always listening to Vin Scully
though he can't hear a thing, just likes to see
his customers soften into smiles when they
hear Vin above the ozone hum of traffic
at the far edge of the San Gabriel Valley
and ask for five dollars worth of regular by
holding up an open hand and mouthing, "Five."
We're sixty miles from the ocean but even
Ricky surfs when he's not cutting grass,
which is what we talk about between sips
of sloe gin in his upstairs garret, the view
of forever falling first on our folks below.
He leans back against his headboard and shapes
the long barrel of perfect Trestles with the one hand
not holding a glass; I say, Yeah, but what about
Rincon, and I whistle the sound of an offshore wind
holding up a long right wrapping around the point.
Ricky's dad could turn a tough cut of antelope
into prime sirloin on the Weber he keeps endlessly
fired at the edge of the driveway beside his garage,
though right now he's working a grill full
of chicken breasts. And Mom, she's slipping loose
this second of any sleepy hold on sweet ruin, her hand
on Dad's forearm, my old man with his can

of Pabst leaning in for an early evening kiss, he
who taught me how to read the beach break
at 56th Street not far from the Rusty Pelican
and all those yachts. "It's Dick Dale's," he says
out of nowhere. "Not David Crosby."
"A Tom Collins!" yells Uncle Sal, Fiona smilling now
at the soft center of this circle of time.

**FOUR**
ACCIDENTAL HAPPINESS

# The Gods

My mother asked me
to take a picture of you.
I think she thinks she
might never meet you,
and I wonder that too.
How do I explain this,
that my mother wants
to believe in you as I do,
to see your face like
a slim trace of moon
surprising an afternoon sky.
Should I ask you to pose
as I pull my phone more
or less casually from my
pocket. Should I say,
"Hold still, my love"
which is like asking my mother
to rise from her wheelchair
and dance? Or should I ask
a friend to watch
for the moment when our
eyes are closed, when you
won't notice the flash of his
phone as my tongue
slides into your mouth and
for seconds like slow hours
we slip our skin and blend
into a single shape: a kiss,
which is how the gods
solved the problem of
separate selves.
My mother would like me
to be less alone. It would
help if she could see
your face.

## Like Light

Where are you now
when what I have instead
is the slow percussion
of raindrops on rhododendron
leaves, the slip
of sunlight from sky
as evening solders
the soft metal
of light into night?
I love you like light.
Like the taste
of air between blue
and blue: the blue
of sky and the blue
of memory, which is
a blue bird made of
glass, a thrush through
which fields and trees
are as visible as a tiny
trembling heart, blue
bird building with
scraps of tin foil
a nest of mirrors.
For two years I turned
my mirrors to the walls.
Today I wrote
*I love you.* Today
I turned the mirrors
around and found
a face I recognized
instead of remembered.

# Aubade (Lisa Lisa Lisa)

Sometimes I kiss the inch
of air above your body
warmed by your skin.
Or I feel your heat
from across the room
where I stand stiff
as a robot in the metallic
air of moonlight, hand flat
against the windowpane
as if to feel light pass
through glass. Why
am I still that robot,
aware of what I can't feel?
If I say your name
three times my voice
becomes a meadowlark's,
not the sad creak
of a mechanical man.
So here I am with wings—
here I am, a robot boy
and his dream of singing.
I watch you sleep and feel
the light cool against
my hand, my hand
that soon will warm itself
with your body
as I search again for what
I know is there:
a tattooed lark sketched
in the curve beneath
your hip, the notes
of a song trailing

around your waist like
the frailest belt,
"hymns at heaven's gate"
that you and I can hear
though only at daybreak
and only as we kiss, preparing
once again to part,
promising to return.
I promise. Please tell me
you promise, too.

# Rowing with Wings

If you are my problem

then my problem is a lot like light:
I can't see it but it's all over everything.

I fell asleep beside you so sure of myself, so certain,
then woke inside *The Circus Animals' Desertion.*

The words were ten feet tall—I stumbled
again and again beside the couplet

*Players and painted stage took all my love,*
*And not those things that they were emblems of.*

But they were letters instead of language,
as tall as trees along the sidewalk.

I left the poem's end alone, so often abused
and known: *Now that my ladder's gone,*

*I must lie down where all the ladders start*
*In the foul rag and bone shop of the heart.*

When I fell asleep certain, I dreamed
you knew me. I woke inside a poem

as true as a smear of moonlight
on your thigh: It meant something,

and then it was gone. I woke a mile
off the coast of the Country of the Young—

I could see it beyond the bed, beyond
your sleeping body. Instead

of waking you, I rowed away, my arms
like wings. I am so tired of rowing away.

# Never in Winter

With three kids the world breaks down
to chicken nuggets:

Walt is 17 and all
for McDonald's, particularly the ten-piece
with a side of fries: "Tempura battered
and cooked to golden perfection," he says
reading from his phone, not surprised
to find the nuggets have their own
Wikipedia page;

while Phoebe, 15, prefers baked
potatoes to French fries, so where else
but Wendy's, regardless of the chicken's
weird texture;

and Dash who's fully five
is surest of all: Burger King and their crown-
shaped nuggets,

then an hour climbing through
the indoor playground, which has a room
to itself off the main dining area, a room
that in winter is Eden and nothing less,
with greasy windows and socks
scattered across the rubber mats.

*

For eight months you've loved me
though never in winter, and I hope
you love me forever. I hope. But still,
until today you haven't spent a Sunday afternoon
reading the paper in the tropical climate
of Burger King's indoor playground,

kids screaming like delirious macaws
as snow drifts against the floor to ceiling
windows and the parking lot turns to silver
cars draped in silver air, the gray wind filled
to overflowing with snow so white it holds
the light in its teeth and makes the gray
world seem like money: silver everywhere.

*

I'm never bored though not for lack of trying.
It's just that a kid's world is stuck in neutral,
the present expanding to the edges of
every room and every body, so that
boredom is beaten back like every
mistake I've ever made, encased in
amber, stored in mason jars, and consigned
to the pantry of the past. We may not
make it home through this blizzard.

*

Walt wanders in from the main dining
room with another order of BK nuggets,
not his favorite but good enough.
Dash is lost in the plastic tubes
overhead, occasionally sliding down
from on high before
climbing back to the top, stopping
at each bubble porthole
to knock loudly and scream for one of us.
And to laugh.

And Phoebe reads by a window, looking up
now and then to compare the world outside
to the words in her book.

She looks over
at me, over at you, back at the page.
Is this it, you think:
a boyfriend with three kids and
two ex-wives in the wings?
I think that too,
though I forget the mistakes
and listen to Dash, suddenly singing
near the ceiling.

*

As good as this is, it would be better
with you, though you're not so sure
about that and don't need to be:
for now we're happy in neutral,
in a moment so vast it may never end.
For now.
You reach across the table for my hand,
your sleeve grazing an open
ketchup packet.
Dash is still singing.
I watch you look up.

# A Morning Milkshake

It's not even 8:30 on a cold
September morning but he's finishing up
a chocolate shake, from the looks of it,
his smile through the diner window
as sticky as my six-year-old's fingers
post-peach, the pit beneath the sofa,
hand prints on his t-shirt. But this guy
is maybe forty, though he's got that vague look
of the nearly homeless, sort of gray
around the eyes, eyes surrounded
by wrinkles now deepened by a smile,
the smile of a man who's just had a milkshake
for breakfast. There's no wreckage
of eggs and bacon on the table
in front of him, no empty bowl of oatmeal.
He took his two bucks into the diner
an hour or so ago and ordered
a chocolate milkshake, drank it
slowly and carefully as he carefully
and slowly read the tossed-off newspaper
he found in the booth when he arrived.
He's now nourished and informed,
now turns to look at me through the window
where I stand on the sidewalk wondering
why in the world I've never had a milkshake
for breakfast. He smiles and waves. I wave back.
Then he returns to his empty glass
and casts around with a spoon for a missed
drip or two, folds the newspaper into thirds
and takes it with him as he leaves the diner,
claps my shoulder as he passes. And I turn
to watch him go, wondering where
in the world, and what next.

# From My Lips

Each night around ten
I stand over my son's bed
for a few minutes and watch
him dream. I usually pull
the blankets closer to his chin
and kiss him before checking
the humidifier and stacking
the books on the floor next
to his bed, the books
he's dragged under the covers.
We all do this, parents.

For years now I've loved
a song by Grant McLennan
called "From My Lips," which
includes the following lines:
"Sometimes it all falls apart
at the seams, and you wish
for the peace of a child's dream."
And I'll admit it, as I kiss
my son and tuck his covers
tight, I think about all that's
fallen apart in our lives

and I lean in close and listen
hard to the dream leaking
from his little body. I let it
change the salt in my life
to sugar, at least for the few
minutes I stand there watching him.
His peace is no more complete
than any I might find, but I
believe in it. That's what
McLennan means I think,
that it's the surrender

that matters, not the treaty
that comes of it, a child's
uncomplicated dream, not
how we interpret it. My son
and I both lost, but he deserves
none of the blame; his peace
has precious little back story;
and so it will save him.
I don't need saving.
I need him. And I'm not
ashamed to say it.

# Accidental Happiness (Auden in Winter)

*St. Mark's Place, 1960*

Is it luck or fated,
willed or created,
the reporter asked,
not hearing himself rhyme.
Auden smiled. Happiness
is an accident, he said.
He hunched
into his topcoat
and looked past
the young man
at a policeman feeding
his horse an apple.
The reporter lowered
his notepad
and looked up.
It was difficult to write
standing outside
on a sidewalk, winter
cramping his fingers.
I meant poetry, he said.
Auden smiled again,
his face, well . . . his face.
He pointed down the street
where the earth seemed
to end in a tangle
of market stalls and old
women—they wheeled
their shopping carts
between rows of vegetables
and discount cleaning
supplies. Happiness
is one door down
from loneliness:

it's easy to enter one
room thinking one is
entering the other.
He didn't say this
out loud; it seemed
silly, even in his mind.
The reporter stared
where Auden
was pointing, not noticing
the great man had turned
around as if to look
at someone who wasn't there.
But had been.